Ms. Terri's CNA Skills Guide For Alabama

Everything You Need To Know To Pass
The Alabama CNA Skills Exam

Terri Walton

TABLE OF CONTENTS

INTRODUCTION

Welcome to *Ms. Terri's CNA Skills Guide for Alabama.* Whether you're preparing for your first CNA exam or returning to refresh your skills, this guide was created to help you succeed with confidence and clarity.

Who This Guide Is For

This book is written for aspiring CNAs in Alabama who want to pass the skills portion of the exam. It's for first-time test takers, returning students who need a refresher, and instructors looking for a dependable classroom resource.

What Makes the Alabama CNA Exam Unique

The CNA skills exam in Alabama includes specific tasks you must perform exactly as trained. Some steps, such as handwashing, carry extra weight and must be demonstrated perfectly. This guide breaks everything down into simple, doable steps so nothing is left to chance.

How to Use This Book

Each chapter walks you through one skill tested on the Alabama CNA exam. You'll see:

- A short introduction explaining why the skill matters

- List of supplies you need

- A friendly, easy-to-follow list of steps (with exact words to say where needed)

- Common mistakes to avoid (×)

- A checklist to help you self-review before moving on (✓)

At the end, you'll find a Final Skills Checklist you can use for quick review before the exam.

Let's begin!

HANDWASHING

Handwashing ensures patient safety and protects you and others from the spread of infection. Mastering this step builds confidence for the rest of the exam.

Supplies Needed

None required

Step-by-Step Instructions

1. Knock and say, "Hello, It's Terri. May I come in? I'm here to demonstrate my handwashing skill. Is now a good time?"

2. Dispense the paper towel.

3. Turn on the water.

4. Wet your hands.

5. Don't shake your hands.

6. Put soap on your hands and lower your hands below your elbows.

7. Lather all surfaces of your hands, fingers, in between fingers, and wrists for twenty seconds. Make sure your hands are always lower than your elbows.

8. After twenty seconds, wash your fingernails.

9. Rinse your hands and your fingernails. Don't shake your hands.

10. Get a clean paper towel and dry your hands.

11. Throw that paper towel in the trash.

12. Get another clean paper towel to turn off the water.

13. Throw that paper towel in the trash without contaminating your hands.

Common Mistakes to Avoid

× Don't shake your hands at any point.

× Don't turn off the faucet with your bare hands.

Skill Complete Checklist

√ Hands always below elbows

√ 20-second lather and nail scrub

√ Dried thoroughly and disposed paper towel

√ Used a clean towel to turn off faucet

Handwashing sets the tone for every skill that follows. Once you master it, you're ready to move confidently into patient care tasks.

PULSE

This skill evaluates your ability to locate the correct pulse site, count accurately for a full minute, and communicate clearly with the proctor. A mistake in timing or communication may result in failure.

Supplies Needed

- Pen
- Watch with a second hand

Step-by-Step Instructions

1. Knock and say, "Hello, it's Terri. May I come in? I'm here to check your pulse. Is now a good time?"

2. Ask, "May I go wash my hands?"

3. Go wash your hands.

4. Place your first two fingers on the thumb side of the resident's wrist, with the palm up.

5. When you begin counting the pulse, say "start" to the proctor.

6. Count the pulse for one full minute using the second hand on the watch.

7. When you finish counting the pulse, say "stop" to the proctor.

8. Give the resident the call light.

9. Ask, "May I go wash my hands?"

10. Go wash your hands.

11. Record the pulse on the paper provided by the proctor.

Common Mistakes to Avoid

× Counting for less than one full minute

× Forgetting to say "start" and "stop"

× Using the thumb instead of fingers

× Recording the result before hand hygiene

Skill Complete Checklist

✓ Washed hands before and after

✓ Located the correct pulse site (thumb side)

✓ Counted for a full minute

✓ Used clear verbal cues ("start" and "stop")

✓ Gave call light and documented correctly

Measuring a resident's pulse helps monitor heart health and detect changes that may require medical attention. Accuracy and timing are critical for this task, and verbal cues must be used clearly for the proctor. Now that you've mastered this, let's move to another vital sign—respirations.

RESPIRATION

This skill checks your ability to accurately observe and count breaths. Respirations must be counted for a full minute and clearly reported.

Supplies Needed

- Pen

- Watch with a second hand

Step-by-Step Instructions

1. Knock and say, "Hello, it's Terri. May I come in? I'm here to check your respirations. Is now a good time?"

2. Ask, "May I go wash my hands?"

3. Go wash your hands.

4. When you begin counting the respirations, say "Start" to the proctor.

5. Count the respirations for one full minute using the second hand on the watch.

6. *Reminder*: one breath in and one breath out is equal to one respiration.

7. When finished counting the respirations, say "Stop" to the proctor.

8. Give the resident the call light.

9. Ask, "May I go wash my hands?"

10. Go wash your hands.

11. Record the respirations on the paper provided by the proctor.

Common Mistakes to Avoid

- × Counting for less than a full minute

- × Forgetting to say "Start" or "Stop"

- × Recording the result before hand hygiene

Skill Complete Checklist

- ✓ Maintained discretion while observing

- ✓ Counted for a full minute

- ✓ Clear verbal cues ("start" and "stop") used

- ✓ Washed hands before and after

Measuring respirations helps detect early signs of distress or illness. With this step complete, you're ready to move into other measurement skills like blood pressure.

BLOOD PRESSURE

This task evaluates your ability to find the brachial pulse, properly place and use the cuff and stethoscope, and accurately measure and report systolic and diastolic readings.

Supplies Needed

- Blood pressure cuff
- Alcohol pads
- Pen
- Stethoscope

Step-by-Step Instructions

1. Knock and say, "Hello, it's Terri. May I come in? I'm here to check your blood pressure. Is now a good time?"

2. Ask, "May I go wash my hands?"

3. Go wash your hands.

4. Clean the earpieces of the stethoscope, the bell, and the diaphragm with an alcohol pad.

5. Start at the resident's pinky finger and use your first two fingers to go up to the bend of the resident's arm to feel for the brachial pulse.

6. Once you feel the brachial pulse, place the blood pressure cuff slightly above the crease of the resident's arm.

7. Make sure the blood pressure cuff is snug on the resident's arm.

8. Line the sensor/arrow up with the resident's pinky finger.

9.   Put the earpieces of the stethoscope in your ears.

10.   With one hand, put the bell of the stethoscope where you felt the brachial pulse.

11.   Use the other hand to hold the bulb and pump the cuff up to 180-200.

12.   Release the air slowly in the cuff. Listen for the first sound and the last sound. The first sound is the systolic (top number) blood pressure; the second sound is the diastolic (bottom number) blood pressure.

13.   Give the resident the call light.

14.   Ask, "May I go wash my hands?"

15.   Go wash your hands.

16.   Record the blood pressure on the paper provided by the proctor.

Common Mistakes to Avoid

×   Placing the cuff too high or too loose

×   Not aligning the sensor properly

×   Forgetting to clean the stethoscope parts

×   Recording readings without confirming both sounds

×   Skipping hand hygiene before or after

Skill Complete Checklist

✓   Cuff positioned properly and snug

✓   Brachial pulse located and bell placed correctly

✓   Cuff pumped to proper range (180–200)

✓   Both systolic and diastolic sounds clearly identified

✓ Equipment cleaned and hands washed before/after

✓ Reading accurately recorded

Accurate blood pressure measurement combines technical accuracy with calm communication. Mastery of this skill is essential for monitoring changes in a resident's health over time.

NAIL CARE

This skill evaluates your ability to perform basic nail care while maintaining infection control and resident comfort. Correct use of tools and respectful communication are critical.

Supplies Needed

- Three towels

- One washcloth

- Nail file

- Lotion

- Bath basin

- Orangewood stick

Step-by-Step Instructions

1. Knock and say, "Hello, it's Terri. May I come in? I'm here to do your nail care. Is now a good time?"

2. Place three towels and one washcloth on the nightstand. Always leave one unused towel on the nightstand for the barrier towel.

3. Ask, "May I go wash my hands?"

4. Go wash your hands.

5. Close the privacy curtains.

6. Close the blinds.

7. Push on the bed to make sure it is locked.

8. Ensure the bed is in the lowest position.

9. Move the overbed table in front of the resident

10. Cover the overbed table with a towel.

11. Place two towels and one washcloth on table.

12. Ask, "May I get your supplies?"

13. Retrieve the lotion, nail file, orangewood stick, and bath basin.

14. Ask, "May I go to your bathroom and get some water?"

15. Verbalize and perform that you are checking the water on the inside of your wrist to confirm that it is not too hot.

16. Place the bath basin on the overbed table.

17. Get a chair to sit in while performing the skill.

18. Put on gloves.

19. Put the resident's hand in the water.

20. Ask, "Is this water temperature okay for you?"

21. Wash the resident's hand and in between their fingers with the washcloth.

22. Place the dirty washcloth on the corner of the overbed table.

23. Dry the resident's hand and in between their fingers with a towel.

24. Place the towel on the overbed table to be used later.

25. Use the "flat side" of the orangewood stick to clean under each fingernail. Wipe the orangewood stick on the towel that the bath basin is sitting on after each fingernail.

26. Wipe the hand/fingernails with the towel you used to dry the hand.

27. File each fingernail with the nail file.

28. Wipe the hand/fingernails with the towel you used to dry the hand.

29. Put lotion in your hands and warm it up by rubbing your hands together.

30. Put lotion on the resident's hand.

31. Ask resident, "Is that okay?"

32. Ask, "May I go to your bathroom?"

33. Take the bath basin to the bathroom.

34. Empty the bath basin in the toilet, rinse, empty in the toilet again, and dry.

35. Ask, "May I put your supplies back?"

36. Place supplies in the dirty area.

37. Gather all dirty linens and place them in the hamper.

38. Remove gloves and place them in the garbage can.

39. Place the overbed table and the chair back.

40. Open the privacy curtains.

41. Open the blinds.

42. Push on the bed to make sure it is locked.

43. Ensure the bed is in the lowest position.

44. Give the resident the call light.

45. Ask, "Do you need anything else?"

46. Ask, "May I go wash my hands?"

47. Go wash your hands.

Common Mistakes to Avoid

- × Forgetting to verbalize temperature check

- × Not maintaining a clean barrier towel

- × Skipping gloves or improper disposal

Skill Complete Checklist

- √ Clean water and barrier towel used

- √ Orangewood stick and nail file handled properly

- √ Resident comfort checked during and after

- √ Hands washed before and after

- √ All supplies returned and area restored

Nail care requires attention to hygiene and gentle technique. Once you master this, you're ready to move on to other personal care tasks, such as mouth care or foot care.

MOUTHCARE

This task evaluates your ability to provide oral hygiene using the correct supplies, protect the resident's clothing, and maintain infection control throughout.

Supplies Needed

- Three towels

- Emesis basin

- Two small cups

- Toothbrush

- Toothpaste

- Mouthwash

Step-by-Step Instructions

1. Knock and say, "Hello, it's Terri. May I come in? I'm here to do your mouth care. Is now a good time?"

2. Place three towels on the nightstand. Always leave one unused towel on the nightstand for the barrier towel.

3. Ask, "May I go wash my hands?"

4. Go wash your hands.

5. Close the privacy curtains.

6. Close the blinds.

7. Push on the bed to make sure it is locked.

8. Ensure the bed is in the lowest position.

9. Move the overbed table to the bedside and cover it with a towel.

10. Ask, "May I get your supplies"?

11. Place one towel on the table.

12. Retrieve the emesis basin, two small cups, a toothbrush, toothpaste, and mouthwash.

13. Ask, "May I go to your bathroom and get some water?"

14. Take two small cups. Fill one full of water and the other one half full of water.

15. Come back and sit the cups on the overbed table. Add the mouthwash to the one that is half-full of water.

16. Raise the head of the bed 45 degrees before you start brushing the resident's teeth.

17. Put on gloves.

18. Ask, "May I drape your shirt?"

19. Drape the resident with a towel.

20. Dip the toothbrush in a full cup of water.

21. Put the toothpaste on the toothbrush.

22. Ask, "May I brush your teeth?"

23. Brush all surfaces of the teeth.

24. Ask, "Can you please stick out your tongue?"

25. Brush the resident's tongue.

26. Ask, "Can you please spit into the emesis basin?"

27. Give the resident a small cup of half water and half mouthwash.

28. Explain, "This is half water and half mouthwash. Please gargle and don't swallow."

29. Ask, "Can you please spit into the emesis basin?"

30. Wipe the resident's mouth with the draped towel and remove.

31. Empty the full cup of water into the emesis basin.

32. Throw away the two small cups.

33. Ask, "May I go to your bathroom?"

34. Take the emesis basin and the toothbrush.

35. Empty the emesis basin in the toilet, rinse, empty it in the toilet again, and dry.

36. Rinse the toothbrush and dry it.

37. Ask, "May I put your supplies back?"

38. Place them in the dirty area.

39. Gather all the dirty linens and place them in the hamper.

40. Remove gloves and place them in the garbage can.

41. Place the overbed table back.

42. Open the privacy curtains.

43. Open the blinds.

44. Push on the bed to make sure it is locked.

45. Ensure the bed is in the lowest position.

46. Give the resident the call light.

47. Ask, "Do you need anything else?"

48. Ask, "May I go wash my hands?"

49. Go wash your hands.

Common Mistakes to Avoid

× Forgetting to raise the head of the bed before brushing

× Using the same towel for multiple purposes

× Not discarding cups or rinsing the emesis basin and toothbrush

× Missing final hand hygiene

Skill Complete Checklist

✓ Supplies gathered and disposed correctly

✓ Gloves used and removed properly

✓ Bed locked and head raised before brushing

✓ Oral care provided thoroughly and respectfully

✓ Final hand hygiene performed

Oral care promotes comfort and prevents infection. Completing this task correctly demonstrates your attention to detail and respect for the resident's well-being.

FOOT CARE

This task evaluates your ability to provide safe and hygienic foot care using proper technique and equipment while ensuring resident comfort and dignity.

Supplies Needed

- Three towels
- Two washcloths
- Soap
- Lotion
- Bath basin

Step-by-Step Instructions

1. Knock and say, "Hello, it's Terri. May I come in? I'm here to do your foot care. Is now a good time?"

2. Place three towels and two washcloths on the nightstand. Always leave one unused towel on the nightstand for the barrier towel.

3. Ask, "May I go wash my hands?"

4. Go wash your hands.

5. Close the privacy curtains.

6. Close the blinds.

7. Push on the bed to ensure it is locked.

8. Ensure the bed is in the lowest position.

9. Fold a towel in half and place it on the floor in front of the resident's chair.

10. Ask, "May I get your supplies?"

11. Retrieve bath basin, soap, and lotion.

12. Place one towel, both washcloths, soap, and lotion on the towel on the floor.

13. Ask, "May I use your bathroom to get some water?"

14. Verbalize and perform that you are checking the water temperature on the inside of your wrist to confirm it's not too hot.

15. Fill the bath basin with water. Place bath basin on towel on floor.

16. Put on gloves.

17. Wet one washcloth, apply soap, and place it on the "clean side" of the basin, i.e., the left side.

18. Wet the second washcloth without soap and place it on the clean side.

19. Lift the bath basin and unfold the towel in front of the resident.

20. Explain that you're about to begin foot care.

21. Remove the resident's shoe and sock.

22. Place the resident's foot in the bath basin.

23. Ask, "Is the water okay?"

24. Lift the resident's foot above the water.

25. Wash the foot thoroughly with the soapy washcloth, including between the toes.

26. Place the soapy washcloth on the "dirty side," i.e., the right side of the basin.

27. Place the foot back into the water.

28. Rinse the foot with the second washcloth, including between the toes.

29. Place the rinse cloth on the dirty side.

30. Remove the foot from the water.

31. Move the basin to the side while keeping it on the towel.

32. Dry the foot completely, including between the toes.

33. Warm lotion in your hands.

34. Apply lotion to the foot, avoiding the areas between the toes.

35. Place used towel on the dirty side.

36. Put the resident's socks and shoes back on.

37. Move the towel from in front of the resident.

38. Ask, "May I go to your bathroom?"

39. Take the bath basin to the bathroom.

40. Empty the basin into the toilet, rinse, empty again, and dry.

41. Ask, "May I put your supplies back?"

42. Place all supplies in the dirty area.

43. Place dirty linens in the hamper.

44. Remove gloves and place them in the garbage can.

45. Open the privacy curtains.

46. Open the blinds.

47. Push on the bed to ensure it is locked.

48. Ensure the bed is in the lowest position.

49. Give the resident the call light.

50. Ask, "Do you need anything else?"

51. Ask, "May I go wash my hands?"

52. Go wash your hands.

Common Mistakes to Avoid

× Applying lotion between the toes

× Skipping drying between the toes

× Not keeping clean and dirty items separate (left and right side respectively)

Skill Complete Checklist

✓ Water temp checked and verbalized

✓ Foot washed and dried, especially between toes

✓ Lotion applied properly (avoiding toes)

✓ Supplies and linens handled correctly

✓ Final hand hygiene completed

Foot care is a simple task that can make a big difference in a resident's comfort and health. Performing it with care shows attention to both detail and dignity.

DENTURE CARE

This task evaluates your ability to clean and handle dentures hygienically and provide gentle mouth care using correct supplies and procedures.

Supplies Needed

- Five towels

- Emesis basin

- Two small cups

- Toothbrush

- Toothpaste

- Mouthwash

- Toothette

Step-by-Step Instructions

Part 1 – Cleaning the Dentures

1. Knock and say, "Hello, it's Terri. May I come in? I'm here to do your denture care. Is now a good time?"

2. Place five towels on the nightstand. Always leave one unused towel on the nightstand for the barrier towel.

3. Ask, "May I go wash my hands?"

4. Go wash your hands.

5. Close the privacy curtains.

6. Close the blinds.

7. Push on the bed to ensure it is locked.

8. Ensure the bed is in the lowest position.

9. Ask, "May I go to your bathroom?"

10. Take two towels to the bathroom—one for the sink counter and one to line the sink.

11. Ask, "May I get your supplies?"

12. Retrieve the dentures, toothbrush, toothpaste, and gloves.

13. Ask, "May I go to your bathroom?"

14. Take the supplies to the bathroom.

15. Put on gloves.

16. Open the denture cup and place dentures on the lid.

17. Empty the cup into the toilet, rinse, empty again, and refill with cool water.

18. Wet the toothbrush and apply toothpaste.

19. Rinse dentures.

20. Brush the top and bottom of the dentures.

21. Rinse dentures again.

22. Place dentures back in the cleaned denture cup.

23. Rinse and dry the toothbrush.

24. Rinse both parts of the lid.

25. Place the lid securely on the cup.

26. Ask, "May I put your supplies back?"

27. Place all supplies in the dirty area.

28. Ask, "May I go to your bathroom?"

29. Place dirty linens in the hamper.

30. Remove gloves and place them in the garbage can.

31. Ask, "May I go wash my hands?"

32. Go wash your hands.

Part 2 – Mouth Care for Denture Wearers

33. Move the overbed table to the bedside and cover it with a towel.

34. Ask, "May I get your supplies?"

35. Retrieve the emesis basin, two small cups, mouthwash, and too-thette.

36. Ask, "May I go to your bathroom?"

37. Fill one small cup with water and one half-full.

38. Add mouthwash to the half-full cup.

39. Place both cups on the overbed table.

40. Put on gloves.

41. Ask, "May I drape your shirt?"

42. Drape the resident with a towel.

43. Dip the toothette in the cup with water and mouthwash.

44. Ask, "May I clean your mouth?"

45. Gently clean the resident's gums, tongue, and lips.

46. Say, "Can you please spit into the emesis basin?"

47. Say, "Here is some water to rinse with."

48. Say, "Can you please spit into the emesis basin?"

49. Wipe the resident's mouth and remove the towel.

50. Empty the remaining mouthwash into the emesis basin.

51. Discard the two cups and toothette.

52. Ask, "May I go to your bathroom?"

53. Take the emesis basin to the bathroom.

54. Empty the emesis basin into the toilet. Rinse, empty again, and dry.

55. Ask, "May I put your supplies back?"

56. Place items in the dirty area.

57. Place dirty linens in the hamper.

58. Remove gloves and place them in the garbage can.

59. Return the overbed table to its original position.

60. Open the privacy curtains.

61. Open the blinds.

62. Push on the bed to ensure it is locked.

63. Ensure the bed is in the lowest position.

64. Give the resident the call light.

65. Ask, "Do you need anything else?"

66. Ask, "May I go wash my hands?"

67. Go wash your hands.

Common Mistakes to Avoid

×   Failing to line the sink with a towel before handling dentures

×   Using hot water in the denture cup

×   Applying too much pressure when brushing dentures

×   Forgetting to clean the resident's gums and tongue

×   Not discarding the toothette or performing hand hygiene after both parts

Skill Complete Checklist

✓   Sink and counter lined with towels

✓   Dentures and toothbrush properly cleaned and stored

✓   Oral care performed respectfully and thoroughly

✓   Gloves used and discarded properly

✓   Final hand hygiene completed

Denture care is essential for oral hygiene and preventing infection in residents who wear dentures. Done with care and respect, it upholds dignity while meeting state requirements.

BEDPAN

This task evaluates your ability to safely and respectfully assist a resident with toileting while maintaining privacy, infection control, and clear communication.

Supplies Needed

- Two towels
- Bedpan

Step-by-Step Instructions

1. Knock and say, "Hello, it's Terri. May I come in? I saw your call light on. Do you need something?"

2. Resident responds: "I need the bedpan."

3. Place two towels on the nightstand. Always leave one unused towel on the nightstand for the barrier towel.

4. Ask, "May I go wash my hands?"

5. Go wash your hands.

6. Close privacy curtains.

7. Close the blinds.

8. Push on the bed to ensure it is locked.

9. Ensure the bed is in the lowest position.

10. Put on gloves.

11. Ask, "May I get out your supplies?"

12. Retrieve the bedpan.

13. Ask, "Can you bend your knees, grab the other side rail, and roll on your side for me?"

14. Place a towel under the resident.

15. Ensure the gown is out of the way.

16. Position the bedpan under the resident, wide end toward the top.

17. Say, "You can roll back over now."

18. Remove gloves and place them in the garbage can.

19. Ask, "May I go wash my hands?"

20. Go wash your hands.

21. Re-enter and say, "I'm going to raise the head of your bed."

22. Raise the head of the bed.

23. Say, "Here is some toilet paper to wipe yourself and some to wipe your hands."

24. Say, "Here is your call light. I'm going to step around the privacy curtain. Please let me know when you are finished."

25. Resident states: "I'm finished."

26. Re-enter and say, "I'm going to let the head of your bed down."

27. Lower the head of the bed.

28. Put on gloves.

29. Take the call light and place it on the bed.

30. Discard toilet paper from the resident.

31. Hold the bedpan in place while the resident rolls to the side.

32. Ask, "Can you bend your knees, grab the other side rail, and roll on your side for me?"

33. Remove the bedpan carefully.

34. Leave the towel under the resident.

35. Say, "You can roll back over now."

36. Ask, "May I go to your bathroom?"

37. Take the bedpan to the bathroom.

38. Empty contents into the toilet, rinse, empty again, and dry.

39. Ask, "May I put your supplies back?"

40. Place the bedpan in the dirty area.

41. Ask, "Can you bend your knees, grab the other side rail, and roll on your side for me?"

42. Retrieve the towel from under the resident.

43. Say, "You can roll back over now."

44. Place dirty linens in the hamper.

45. Remove gloves and place them in the garbage can.

46. Ask, "May I go wash my hands?"

47. Open privacy curtains.

48. Open the blinds.

49. Push on the bed to ensure it is locked.

50. Ensure the bed is in the lowest position.

51. Give the resident the call light.

52. Ask, "Do you need anything else?"

53. Ask, "May I go wash my hands?

54. Go wash your hands.

Common Mistakes to Avoid

× Placing the bedpan incorrectly (wide end toward feet)

× Not holding the bedpan while the resident rolls

× Forgetting to raise the head of the bed after placing the bedpan

× Skipping handwashing or glove removal steps

Skill Complete Checklist

√ Bedpan placed correctly and securely

√ Resident positioned safely and comfortably

√ Hands washed and gloves changed as needed

√ Bedpan emptied and cleaned properly

√ Resident given call light and final care

Helping a resident use a bedpan with dignity is part of compassionate care. It highlights your ability to balance clinical hygiene with personal respect.

CATHETER CARE

Catheter care is crucial for preventing urinary tract infections and ensuring resident comfort. This skill demonstrates your ability to clean the surrounding area and the catheter tubing with precision and sensitivity.

Supplies Needed

- Four towels
- Five washcloths
- Bath basin
- Soap

Step-by-Step Instructions

1. Knock and say, "Hello, it's Terri. May I come in? I'm here to do your catheter care. Is now a good time?"

2. Place three towels and five washcloths on the nightstand. Always leave one unused towel on the nightstand for the barrier towel.

3. Ask, "May I go wash my hands?"

4. Go wash your hands.

5. Close the privacy curtains.

6. Close the blinds.

7. Push on the bed to ensure it is locked.

8. Make sure the bed is in the lowest position.

9. Move the overbed table to the bedside and cover it with a towel.

10. Place two towels and five washcloths on the left side of the table (clean side).

11. Ask, "May I get your supplies?"

12. Retrieve the bath basin and soap. Place soap on the clean side.

13. Ask, "May I use your bathroom to get some water?"

14. Verbalize and perform that you are checking the water on the inside of your wrist to confirm that it is not too hot.

15. Place the basin in the center of the table.

16. Put on gloves.

17. Wet two washcloths, apply soap, and place them on the clean side of the basin.

18. Explain to the resident that you are starting catheter care.

19. Pull back the gown and place a towel under the resident.

20. Pick up a soapy washcloth and touch the resident.

21. Ask, "Is the water okay?"

22. Using the same soapy washcloth, spread the labia and wipe down the side furthest from you.

23. Flip the cloth, wipe down the side closest to you.

24. Place the washcloth on the right side (dirty side).

25. Dip a clean washcloth in water, spread the labia, and rinse the side furthest from you.

26. Flip, rinse the side nearest you.

27. Place the rinse cloth on the dirty side.

28. Use a clean towel, spread the labia, and dry the furthest side.

29. Flip, dry the nearest side.

30. Place a towel on the dirty side.

Catheter Tubing

31. Hold the catheter at the top to avoid pulling.

32. Use a soapy washcloth to wipe all the way down the tubing.

33. Flip and wipe again.

34. Place the washcloth on the dirty side.

35. Dip a clean washcloth in water and rinse all the way down.

36. Flip and rinse again.

37. Place on the dirty side.

38. Use a clean washcloth to dry all the way down.

39. Flip and dry again.

40. Place the washcloth on the dirty side.

41. Remove the towel from under the resident and place it on the dirty side.

42. Cover the resident.

43. Ask, "May I go to your bathroom?"

44. Take a bath basin to the bathroom.

45. Empty the basin into the toilet. Rinse, empty again, and dry.

46. Ask, "May I put your supplies back?"

47. Place supplies in the dirty area.

48. Place dirty linens in the hamper.

49. Remove gloves and place them in the garbage can.

50. Ask, "May I go wash my hands?"

51. Go wash your hands.

52. Open the privacy curtains.

53. Open the blinds.

54. Push on the bed to ensure it is locked.

55. Ensure the bed is in the lowest position.

56. Give the resident the call light.

57. Ask, "Do you need anything else?"

58. Ask, "May I go wash my hands?"

59. Go wash your hands.

Common Mistakes to Avoid

- × Not holding the catheter tubing during cleaning
- × Using the same washcloth section for both sides
- × Forgetting to check the water temperature aloud
- × Applying lotion or powder near the catheter site (if attempted)

Skill Complete Checklist

- ✓ Clean and dirty areas clearly separated
- ✓ Labia cleaned and dried separately on each side
- ✓ Catheter tubing washed, rinsed, and dried correctly
- ✓ Gown repositioned and resident covered
- ✓ Final hand hygiene performed

Catheter care prevents infection and protects resident safety. Careful technique here reflects your professionalism and attention to detail.

EMPTY URINARY DRAINAGE BAG

Emptying a urinary drainage bag helps monitor fluid output and prevent infection. This task evaluates your ability to safely empty, measure, and document urine output.

Supplies Needed

- Three towels

- Clear beaker

Step-by-Step Instructions

1. Knock and say, "Hello, it's Terri. May I come in? I'm here to empty your drainage bag. Is now a good time?"

2. Place three towels on the nightstand. Always leave one unused towel on the nightstand for the barrier towel.

3. Ask, "May I go wash my hands?"

4. Go wash your hands.

5. Close the privacy curtains.

6. Close the blinds.

7. Push on the bed to ensure it is locked.

8. Ensure the bed is in the lowest position.

9. Put on gloves.

10. Move the overbed table to the bedside and cover it with a towel.

11. Ask, "May I get your supplies?"

12. Retrieve the clear beaker.

13. Place a towel on the floor under the urinary drainage bag.

14. Open the clamp and empty the bag into the beaker, avoiding splashing.

15. Close the clamp when finished.

16. Place the beaker on the overbed table.

17. Measure the urine at eye level and note the amount in cc's.

18. Do not allow your gloved hand to touch your body during this step.

19. Ask, "May I go to your bathroom?"

20. Take the beaker to the bathroom.

21. Empty the urine into the toilet, rinse the beaker, empty again, and dry.

22. Ask, "May I put your supplies back?"

23. Return supplies to the dirty area.

24. Gather dirty linens and place them in the hamper.

25. Remove gloves and place them in the garbage can.

26. Ask, "May I go wash my hands?"

27. Go wash your hands.

28. Return the overbed table to its original position.

29. Open the privacy curtains.

30. Open the blinds.

31. Push on the bed to ensure it is locked.

32. Ensure the bed is in the lowest position.

33. Give the resident the call light.

34. Ask, "Do you need anything else?"

35. Ask, "May I go wash my hands?"

36. Go wash your hands.

37. Record the urine output in cc's on the proctor's sheet.

Common Mistakes to Avoid

× Touching the inside of the beaker or the drainage port

× Measuring without placing the beaker on a flat surface at eye level

× Forgetting to record urine output

× Skipping hand hygiene after glove removal

Skill Complete Checklist

√ Urine drained without contamination

√ Output measured at eye level and verbalized

√ Measurement recorded correctly

√ Gloves removed and hands washed after procedure

√ Resident given final care and call light

Accurate measurement and clean handling during this task help prevent infection and ensure proper health monitoring. Mastery of this skill shows attention to both detail and safety.

PERINEAL CARE

Perineal care is critical for preventing infections, maintaining hygiene, and ensuring patient dignity. This skill shows your ability to use appropriate cleaning motions and separate surfaces for each area.

Supplies Needed

- Five towels
- Four washcloths
- Bath basin
- Soap

Step-by-Step Instructions

1. Knock and say, "Hello, it's Terri. May I come in? I'm here to do your perineal care. Is now a good time?"

2. Place five towels and four washcloths on the nightstand. Always leave one unused towel on the nightstand for the barrier towel.

3. Ask, "May I go wash my hands?"

4. Go wash your hands.

5. Close privacy curtains.

6. Close the blinds.

7. Push on the bed to ensure it is locked.

8. Ensure the bed is in the lowest position.

9. Move the overbed table to the bedside and cover with a towel.

10. Place three towels and four washcloths on the left side of the table (clean side).

11. Ask, "May I get your supplies?"

12. Retrieve the bath basin and soap. Place soap on the clean side.

13. Ask, "May I use your bathroom to get some water?"

14. Verbalize and perform that you are checking the water on the inside of your wrist to confirm it is not too hot.

15. Place the basin in the center of the table.

16. Put on gloves.

17. Wet two washcloths, apply soap, and place on the clean side of the basin.

18. Explain that you are beginning perineal care.

19. Pull back the resident's gown and place a towel under them.

20. Touch the resident with the washcloth and ask, "Is the water okay?"

Cleaning the Front (Perineal Area)

21. With a soapy washcloth, use four corners to wash:
    a. Corner 1 – Right groin (downward swipe)
    b. Corner 2 – Left groin (downward swipe)
    c. Corner 3 – Inside right labia (downward swipe)
    d. Corner 4 – Inside left labia (downward swipe)

22. Place soiled washcloth on dirty, i.e., the right side.

23. With a clean, wet washcloth, repeat the four-corner technique to rinse in the same order.

24. Place used rinse cloth on the dirty side.

25. To dry, go front to back, flip the towel, and repeat. Never pat dry.

26. Place towel on the dirty side.

27. Cleaning the Back (Buttocks)

28. Ask, "Can you bend your knees, grab the side rail, and roll on your side for me?"

29. With a soapy washcloth, clean bottom front to back, flip, and repeat.

30. Place washcloth on the dirty side.

31. Rinse with a clean, wet washcloth, front to back, flip, and repeat.

32. Place rinse cloth on the dirty side.

33. Dry with a clean towel, front to back, flip, and repeat.

34. Place towel on the dirty side.

35. Say, "You can roll back over now."

36. Remove towel from under resident and place on the dirty side.

37. Cover the resident.

Final Cleanup

38. Ask, "May I go to your bathroom?"

39. Take bath basin to bathroom.

40. Empty into toilet, rinse, empty again, and dry.

41. Ask, "May I put your supplies back?"

42. Place supplies in the dirty area.

43. Place dirty linens in hamper.

44. Remove gloves and place them in the garbage can.

45. Ask, "May I go wash my hands?"

46. Go wash your hands.

47. Open privacy curtains.

48. Open the blinds.

49. Push on the bed to ensure it is locked.

50. Ensure the bed is in the lowest position.

51. Give the resident the call light.

52. Ask, "Do you need anything else?"

53. Ask, "May I go wash my hands?"

54. Go wash your hands.

Common Mistakes to Avoid

× Using the same side of the washcloth for multiple areas

× Not wiping front to back on both front and back sides

× Skipping the towel barrier

× Failing to check water temperature verbally

Skill Complete Checklist

✓ Front and back cleaned with correct order and technique

✓ Clean and dirty areas maintained

✓ Gloves removed and hands washed

✓ Resident covered and call light returned

✓ Supplies disposed of properly

This skill reflects competence and compassion in personal care, and hence, must be done with attention to dignity, comfort, and infection control.

FEEDING

Feeding evaluates your ability to provide appropriate, respectful care while ensuring proper positioning, hygiene, and resident engagement. It also checks whether you confirm the diet and identity before feeding.

Supplies Needed

- Towel

- Clothing protector

- Feeding tray with plate and cup

- Dietary card

- Utensils

Step-by-Step Instructions

1. Knock and say, "Hello, it's Terri. May I come in? I'm here to feed you. Is now a good time?"

2. Place the towel and clothing protector on the nightstand. Always leave one unused towel on the nightstand for the barrier towel.

3. Put the tray on the overbed table.

4. Ask, "May I go wash my hands?"

5. Go wash your hands.

6. Close privacy curtains.

7. Close the blinds.

8. Push on the bed to ensure it is locked.

9. Ensure the bed is in the lowest position.

10. Wipe the resident's hands with a tissue.

11. Apply the clothing protector.

12. Push the overbed table close to the resident.

13. Get a chair and sit at eye level with the resident.

14. Pick up the dietary card.

15. Ask, "Can you state your name for me?"

16. Confirm that the name and diet match the card.

17. Say, "I have some fruit cocktail and water for you. Would you like some?"

18. Feed one spoonful of fruit cocktail.

19. Ask, "Are you done chewing and have you swallowed it?"

20. Ask, "Would you like another bite?"

21. Ask, "Would you like a drink?"

22. Repeat the process until the resident indicates they are done.

23. Move the table and chair back.

24. Wipe the resident's hands and mouth using the clothing protector.

25. Remove the clothing protector.

26. Put the tray in the dirty area.

27. Place dirty linens in the hamper.

28. Open the privacy curtains.

29. Open the blinds.

30. Push on the bed to ensure it is locked.

31. Ensure the bed is in the lowest position.

32. Give the resident the call light.

33. Ask, "Do you need anything else?"

34. Ask, "May I go wash my hands?"

35. Go wash your hands.

36. Record the percentage of the resident who ate and drank on the form provided by the proctor.

Common Mistakes to Avoid

×   Not verifying resident's identity before feeding

×   Not sitting at eye level with resident

×   Feeding too quickly or without checking for swallowing

×   Forgetting to record the intake percentage

Skill Complete Checklist

√   Identity and diet verified

√   Resident sat upright and positioned correctly

√   Hygiene maintained before and after feeding

√   Resident fed respectfully and patiently

√   Intake recorded accurately

Feeding is about more than nutrition; it's about care, communication, and patience.

REPOSITIONING

Repositioning helps prevent bed sores, improves circulation, and enhances comfort for residents. This task evaluates your ability to safely reposition a resident, use appropriate support devices, maintain correct alignment, and communicate respectfully.

Supplies Needed

- Two pillows

- One wedge

Step-by-Step Instructions

1. Knock and say, "Hello, it's Terri. May I come in? I'm here to reposition you. Is now a good time?"

2. Place the wedge and two pillows on the overbed table.

3. Ask, "May I go wash my hands?"

4. Go wash your hands.

5. Close the privacy curtains.

6. Close the blinds.

7. Push on the bed to ensure it is locked.

8. Ensure the bed is in the lowest position.

9. Lower the side rail closest to you.

10. Ask, "Can you bend your knees, grab the other side rail, and roll on your side for me?"

11. Place the wedge behind the resident's back, just above the buttocks, for support.

12. Pick up the first pillow and say, "Can I place this between your ankles and knees?"

13. Position the pillow between the resident's ankles and knees, making sure feet are not stacked and knees are separated.

14. Pick up the second pillow and say, "Can I place your arms on this pillow?"

15. Place the resident's arms on the pillow, ensuring the arms are not stacked.

16. Raise the side rail back up.

17. Return the overbed table to its original position.

18. Open the privacy curtains.

19. Open the blinds.

20. Push on the bed to ensure it is locked.

21. Ensure the bed is in the lowest position.

22. Give the resident the call light.

23. Ask, "Do you need anything else?"

24. Ask, "May I go wash my hands?"

25. Go wash your hands.

Common Mistakes to Avoid

    × Forgetting to align the resident's body properly

    × Stacking the feet or knees

    × Failing to use the wedge or misplacing it

    × Not lowering or raising the side rail appropriately

Skill Complete Checklist

✓ Resident positioned on side with wedge for support

✓ Pillow placed between knees and ankles

✓ Arms supported and not stacked

✓ Side rail lowered and raised correctly

✓ Hands washed before and after

Repositioning isn't just about movement, but also about comfort, safety, and preventing complications. Performing this skill well shows attention to resident dignity and physical care.

DRESSING A RESIDENT WITH A WEAK ARM

Dressing a resident evaluates your ability to dress a resident while protecting the weak arm, using proper technique to ensure safety, comfort, and dignity.

Supplies Needed

- Two towels

- Two shirts

- One pair of socks

- One pair of pants

Step-by-Step Instructions

1. Knock and say, "Hello, it's Terri. May I come in? I'm here to get you dressed. Is now a good time?"

2. Place the clothes and linens on the nightstand. Always leave one unused towel on the nightstand for the barrier towel.

3. Ask, "May I go wash my hands?"

4. Go wash your hands.

5. Close the privacy curtains.

6. Close the blinds.

7. Push on the bed to ensure it is locked.

8. Ensure the bed is in the lowest position.

9. Move the overbed table to the bedside and cover it with a towel.

10. Place the clothing items on the overbed table.

11. Ask, "What color shirt would you like to wear today?"

12. Explain to the resident that you are about to begin dressing them.

13. Put on the resident's socks.

14. Put on the resident's pants, one leg at a time, as far up as possible.

15. Say, "I'm going to cross your arms and roll you over to your side."

16. Roll the resident and pull up pants on one side.

17. Say, "I'm going to roll you to your other side."

18. Roll the resident and pull pants all the way up.

19. Say, "Now I'm going to roll you onto your back."

20. Undress the gown from the strong arm first.

21. Then undress the weak arm.

22. Leave the gown on the chest for dignity.

23. Dress the weak arm first in the new shirt.

24. Say, "I'm going to roll you on your side again."

25. Tuck the shirt under the resident's back.

26. Say, "I'm going to roll you back. Can you please put your other arm in the sleeve?"

27. Complete shirt dressing and button the shirt.

28. Gather all dirty linens and place in the hamper.

29. Return the overbed table to its original position.

30. Open the privacy curtains.

31. Open the blinds.

32. Push on the bed to ensure it is locked.

33. Ensure the bed is in the lowest position.

34. Give the resident the call light in their strong hand.

35. Ask, "Do you need anything else?"

36. Ask, "May I go wash my hands?"

37. Go wash your hands.

Common Mistakes to Avoid

× Dressing the strong arm before the weak arm

× Removing the gown from the weak arm first

× Failing to offer clothing choices

× Not checking bed safety or side rails during turns

Skill Complete Checklist

√ Resident dressed starting with weak arm

√ Gown removed strong arm first

√ Pants and shirt applied with proper body mechanics

√ Call light in strong hand

√ Final hygiene and privacy restored

To sum up, helping a resident dress respectfully and carefully builds trust and supports their independence. It also demonstrates your ability to follow procedure.

RANGE OF MOTION (HIP, KNEE, AND ANKLE)

Range of motion exercises help maintain joint flexibility, reduce stiffness, and prevent contractures. This skill demonstrates your ability to safely support and move a resident's limbs while monitoring for discomfort.

Supplies Needed

- None

Step-by-Step Instructions

1. Knock and say, "Hello, it's Terri. May I come in? I'm here to do range of motion on your hip, knee, and ankle. Is now a good time?"

2. Ask, "May I go wash my hands?"

3. Go wash your hands.

4. Close the privacy curtains.

5. Close the blinds.

6. Push on the bed to ensure it is locked.

7. Ensure the bed is in the lowest position.

Hip and Knee

8. Say, "I'm going to put one hand under your knee and one under your ankle. I'll bend your leg towards your chest three times. If anything hurts or feels uncomfortable, let me know."

9. Place one hand under the resident's knee and one under the ankle.

10. Gently bend the resident's knee toward the chest and return to the bed. Repeat three times.

11. Say, "1, 2—are you okay? 3."

Ankle

12. Say, "Now I'm going to put one hand under your heel and the other under the palm of your foot. I'll bend your foot toward your chest and back three times. Please let me know if anything hurts."

13. Support under the heel and under the foot.

14. Gently dorsiflex and plantarflex the foot three times.

15. Say, "1, 2—are you okay? 3."

Final Steps

16. Open the privacy curtains.

17. Open the blinds.

18. Push on the bed to ensure it is locked.

19. Ensure the bed is in the lowest position.

20. Give the resident the call light.

21. Ask, "Do you need anything else?"

22. Ask, "May I go wash my hands?"

23. Go wash your hands.

Common Mistakes to Avoid

× Moving joints too quickly or forcefully

× Failing to provide verbal cues and comfort checks

× Not supporting both joints during movement

× Omitting privacy or hand hygiene steps

Skill Complete Checklist

√ Supported both joints during movements

√ Moved limb slowly and smoothly

√ Checked for pain or discomfort mid-reps

√ Maintained resident privacy and comfort

√ Washed hands before and after

Range of motion helps residents stay mobile and pain-free. Doing it properly shows your attention to physical care and communication.

RANGE OF MOTION SHOULDER

Shoulder range of motion helps maintain flexibility and reduces the risk of joint stiffness. This skill tests your ability to safely support and move the resident's arm while checking for discomfort.

Supplies Needed

- None

Step-by-Step Instructions

1. Knock and say, "Hello, it's Terri. May I come in? I'm here to do range of motion on your shoulder. Is now a good time?"

2. Ask, "May I go wash my hands?"

3. Go wash your hands.

4. Close the privacy curtains.

5. Close the blinds.

6. Push on the bed to ensure it is locked.

7. Ensure the bed is in the lowest position.

Shoulder – Flexion and Extension

8. Say, "I'm going to put one hand under your wrist and one under your elbow. I'll raise your arm up to ear level three times. Let me know if anything is uncomfortable."

9. Place one hand under the wrist and the other under the elbow.

10. Raise the resident's arm up to ear level.

11. Lower the arm gently.

12. Say: "1, 2—are you okay? 3."

Shoulder – Abduction and Adduction

13. Say, "Now I'm going to move your arm out to the side and back in three times. Please let me know if you feel any discomfort."

14. Gently move the arm out away from the body (abduction) and back in (adduction).

15. Say, "1, 2—are you okay? 3."

Final Steps

16. Open the privacy curtains.

17. Open the blinds.

18. Push on the bed to ensure it is locked.

19. Ensure the bed is in the lowest position.

20. Give the resident the call light.

21. Ask, "Do you need anything else?"

22. Ask, "May I go wash my hands?"

23. Go wash your hands.

Common Mistakes to Avoid

× Not supporting both wrist and elbow

× Moving too quickly or forcefully

× Failing to ask about pain or discomfort mid-reps

× Omitting steps like closing privacy curtains or final handwashing

Skill Complete Checklist

√ Wrist and elbow supported throughout

✓ Arm moved slowly with full range (up/down, out/in)

✓ Checked for discomfort

✓ Maintained privacy and hand hygiene

Shoulder range of motion keeps the joint healthy and functional. Performing this skill carefully reflects your attention to detail and resident safety.

RANGE OF MOTION WRIST AND ELBOW

This task evaluates your ability to assist the resident with controlled, gentle motion in the elbow and wrist, while checking for pain or discomfort.

Supplies Needed

- None

Step-by-Step Instructions

1. Knock and say, "Hello, it's Terri. May I come in? I'm here to do range of motion on your wrist and elbow. Is now a good time?"

2. Ask, "May I go wash my hands?"

3. Go wash your hands.

4. Close the privacy curtains.

5. Close the blinds.

6. Push on the bed to ensure it is locked.

7. Ensure the bed is in the lowest position.

Elbow – Flexion and Extension

8. Say, "I'm going to put my hand under your wrist and my other hand under your elbow. I'm going to bend your arm upwards three times. If it gives you any trouble, please let me know.

9. Support the resident's wrist and elbow.

10. Gently bend the elbow to raise the forearm.

11. Return arm to resting position.

12. Repeat three times. Say, "1, 2—are you okay? 3."

Wrist – Flexion and Extension

13. Say, "Now I'm going to put my hand under your fingers and your wrist, and I'm going to bend your hand back and forth three times. Let me know if anything is uncomfortable."

14. Support the wrist and fingers.

15. Gently bend wrist back (extension) and forward (flexion).

16. Repeat three times. Say, "1, 2—are you okay? 3."

Final Steps

17. Open the privacy curtains

18. Open the blinds.

19. Push on the bed to ensure it is locked.

20. Ensure the bed is in the lowest position.

21. Give the resident the call light.

22. Ask, "Do you need anything else?"

23. Ask, "May I go wash my hands?"

24. Go wash your hands.

Common Mistakes to Avoid

×   Not supporting both wrist and elbow

×   Rushing through the reps

×   Forgetting to ask about pain or discomfort

×   Omitting closing hand hygiene

Skill Complete Checklist

✓ Elbow moved slowly and supported

✓ Wrist moved through full flexion and extension

✓ Checked for discomfort

✓ Maintained privacy, safety, and hand hygiene

Skill Wrap-Up

This skill demonstrates gentleness, awareness, and rhythm. By supporting the resident's joints and asking the right questions, you show that you're paying attention to both safety and comfort.

BED BATH

A bed bath helps maintain hygiene and comfort for residents unable to bathe independently. This skill demonstrates your ability to clean, rinse, and dry the resident's upper body.

Supplies Needed

- Six towels

- Six washcloths

- One sheet

- One gown

- Bath basin

- Soap

- Lotion

Step-by-Step Instructions

1. Knock and say, "Hello, it's Terri. May I come in? I'm here to do your bed bath. Is now a good time?"

2. Place six towels, six washcloths, one sheet, and one gown on the nightstand. Always leave one unused towel on the nightstand for the barrier towel.

3. Ask, "May I go wash my hands?"

4. Go wash your hands.

5. Close privacy curtains.

6. Close the blinds.

7. Push on the bed to ensure it is locked.

8. Ensure the bed is in the lowest position.

9. Move the overbed table to the bedside and cover it with a towel.

10. Place four towels, six washcloths, one sheet, and one gown on the clean side (left) of the table.

11. Ask, "May I get your supplies?"

12. Retrieve bath basin, soap, and lotion. Place soap and lotion on clean side.

13. Place bath basin in the center of the table.

14. Explain to the resident: "I'm going to place this sheet over you, then remove your gown underneath."

15. Undress the resident under the sheet. Place gown on the dirty (right) side.

16. Ask, "May I go use your bathroom to get some water?"

17. Verbalize and perform that you are checking the water on the inside of your wrist to confirm that the water is not too hot.

18. Place bath basin in the center of the table.

19. Put on gloves.

20. Wet two washcloths, apply soap, and place on clean side.

21. Place a towel under the resident's nearest arm.

22. Dip a dry washcloth in water, touch the resident, and ask, "Is the water okay?"

23. Explain: "I'm going to begin your bed bath now."

Face

24. Use one corner of a clean, wet washcloth to clean the eye farthest from you (inner to outer).

25. Use a different corner to clean the other eye (inner to outer).

26. Place used cloth on dirty side.

27. Use another clean washcloth to wash the resident's face.

28. Place it on the dirty side.

29. Dry the face with a clean towel.

30. Place the towel on the dirty side.

Neck, Hand, Arm, Chest, Abdomen

31. Use soapy washcloth to wash the neck, hand, arm, chest, and abdomen.

32. Place used washcloth on the dirty side.

33. Use a clean wet washcloth to rinse same areas.

34. Place used washcloth on the dirty side.

35. Dry the washed areas with a towel.

36. Place towel on the dirty side.

Back

37. Ask, "Can you bend your knees, grab the rail, and roll onto your side for me?"

38. Readjust towel to be under the resident's back.

39. Use soapy washcloth to wash back.

40. Place washcloth on the dirty side.

41. Rinse with clean wet washcloth.

42. Place washcloth on the dirty side.

43. Dry back with a towel.

44. Place towel on the dirty side.

45. Warm lotion in hands and apply to the resident's back.

46. Remove towel from under back and place on the dirty side.

47. Ask, "Can you roll back over for me?"

Finish

48. Dress the resident in a clean gown.

49. Remove the sheet and place it on the dirty side.

50. Ask, "May I go to your bathroom?"

51. Take bath basin to bathroom and empty into toilet. Rinse, empty again, and dry.

52. Ask, "May I put your supplies back?"

53. Return supplies to dirty area.

54. Place dirty linens in hamper.

55. Remove gloves and place them in the garbage can.

56. Open privacy curtains.

57. Open blinds.

58. Push on bed to ensure it is locked.

59. Ensure the bed is in the lowest position.

60. Give the call light to the resident.

61. Ask, "Do you need anything else?"

62. Ask, "May I go wash my hands?"

63. Go wash your hands.

Common Mistakes to Avoid

- × Failing to check water temperature verbally

- × Using same washcloth area on multiple parts

- × Skipping lotion or gown after bath

- × Not supporting dignity with sheet and draping

Skill Complete Checklist

- ✓ Face and upper body washed, rinsed, and dried

- ✓ Back cleaned and lotion applied

- ✓ Clean gown put on

- ✓ Supplies and linens disposed correctly

- ✓ Hands washed before and after

A good bed bath is about more than hygiene. Proper technique shows attention to the resident's comfort and care.

MAKING AN OCCUPIED BED

Keeping a resident's bed clean and comfortable demonstrates your ability to change bed linens with the resident still in bed, without causing discomfort or breaking infection control protocol.

Supplies Needed

- One fitted sheet
- One top sheet
- One pillowcase
- Two towels

Step-by-Step Instructions

1. Knock and say, "Hello, it's Terri. May I come in? I'm here to make your bed. Is now a good time?"

2. Place linens on the nightstand. Always leave one unused towel on the nightstand for the barrier towel.

3. Ask, "May I go wash my hands?"

4. Go wash your hands.

5. Close privacy curtains.

6. Close the blinds.

7. Push on the bed to ensure it is locked.

8. Ensure the bed is in the lowest position.

9. Move the overbed table to the bedside and cover it with a towel.

10. Place fitted sheet, top sheet, and pillowcase on the left side of the table (clean side).

11. Put on gloves.

Changing the Fitted Sheet

12. Ask, "Can you bend your knees, grab the side rail, and roll to your side for me?"

13. Reposition the pillow under the resident's head.

14. Remove fitted sheet from the side closest to you.

15. Place new fitted sheet on that side and tuck it under the dirty one.

16. Raise the side rail.

17. Move overbed table to other side.

18. Lower the opposite side rail.

19. Ask, "Can you bend your knees and roll again?"

20. Reposition the pillow again.

21. Remove the dirty fitted sheet fully and place it on the dirty (right) side of the table.

22. Pull clean sheet fully across and finish tucking.

23. Raise side rail.

24. Return overbed table to original side.

25. Lower side rail.

26. Ask, "Can you roll back over for me?"

Changing the Top Sheet and Pillowcase

27. Remove top sheet without exposing the resident.

28. Replace with clean top sheet.

29. Place dirty top sheet on dirty side of table.

30. Tuck in clean top sheet neatly at the bottom—ensure it's not dragging.

31. Tell the resident, "I'm going to get your pillow."

32. Remove old pillowcase.

33. Place pillow on resident's chest.

34. Turn new pillowcase inside out, insert arm, and pull it over the pillow.

35. Say, "I'm placing the pillow back under your head."

36. Reposition pillow under head.

Final Steps

37. Place all dirty linens in the hamper.

38. Remove gloves and place them in the garbage can.

39. Move overbed table back to its original position.

40. Open the privacy curtains.

41. Open the blinds.

42. Push on the bed to ensure it is locked.

43. Ensure the bed is in the lowest position.

44. Give the resident the call light.

45. Ask, "Do you need anything else?"

46. Ask, "May I go wash my hands?"

47. Go wash your hands.

Common Mistakes to Avoid

× Not keeping the resident covered when changing top sheet

× Letting linens touch the floor

× Forgetting to check bed lock before and after

×   Reaching across resident instead of moving side to side

Skill Complete Checklist

✓ Dirty sheets removed and replaced without exposing resident

✓ Bed stayed locked and low throughout

✓ Clean linens applied correctly and tucked properly

✓ Pillow changed using correct technique

✓ Hands washed before and after

Making an occupied bed requires care and coordination. Doing it right shows your ability to combine comfort, cleanliness, and control under pressure

TRANSFER BED TO CHAIR

Helping a resident safely move from bed to wheelchair is a fundamental caregiving task. This skill demonstrates your ability to transfer with proper body mechanics, clear communication, and equipment use.

Supplies Needed

- Gait belt

- Wheelchair

- Shoes

Step-by-Step Instructions

1. Knock and say, "Hello, it's Terri. May I come in? I'm here to put you in your wheelchair. Is now a good time?"

2. Ask, "May I go wash my hands?"

3. Go wash your hands.

4. Close the privacy curtains.

5. Close the blinds.

6. Push on the bed to ensure it is locked.

7. Ensure the bed is in the lowest position.

8. Place the wheelchair parallel to the bed.

9. Lock the wheelchair wheels.

10. Ask, "Can you please sit on the side of the bed for me?"

11. Put shoes on the resident.

12. Say, "The shoes are on, and the feet are planted on the floor."

13. Ask, "May I get your supplies?"

14. Retrieve the gait belt.

15. Place gait belt on the resident.

16. Make sure the gait belt is snug and flat and not twisted.

17. Position your right knee inside and left leg outside the resident's right leg.

18. Hold the gait belt with palms up, one hand on each side.

19. Say, "We're going to rock back and forth three times. On the third rock, I'll help you stand."

20. Count: "1… 2… 3." Stand the resident.

21. Ask, "Are you okay?"

22. Say, "Now I need you to turn and have a seat."

23. Continue holding the gait belt with palms up as the resident sits.

24. Remove the gait belt.

25. Ask, "May I put your supplies back?"

26. Place the gait belt in the dirty area.

27. Open the privacy curtains.

28. Open the blinds.

29. Push on the bed to ensure it is locked.

30. Ensure the bed is in the lowest position.

31. Give the resident the call light.

32. Ask, "Do you need anything else?"

33. Ask, "May I go wash my hands?"

34. Go wash your hands.

Common Mistakes to Avoid

× Not locking the wheelchair

× Placing gait belt incorrectly or too loose

× Standing without proper knee positioning

× Letting go of the belt while transferring

Skill Complete Checklist

✓ Shoes secured before transfer

✓ Wheelchair positioned and locked

✓ Gait belt placed and held correctly

✓ Resident assisted safely into chair

✓ Hands washed before and after

Proper transfers protect both you and the resident. A smooth and safe transition demonstrates skillful equipment use, clear communication, and prevents injury.

AMBULATION

Walking residents helps improve their circulation, digestion, and mood. This skill shows your ability to safely assist a resident with walking using a gait belt and proper body mechanics.

Supplies Needed

- Gait belt
- Shoes

Step-by-Step Instructions

1. Knock and say, "Hello, it's Terri. May I come in? I'm here to take you for a walk. Is now a good time?"

2. Ask, "May I go wash my hands?"

3. Go wash your hands.

4. Close the privacy curtains.

5. Close the blinds.

6. Push on the bed to ensure it is locked.

7. Ensure the bed is in the lowest position.

8. Place shoes on the resident.

9. Say, "The shoes are on, and the feet are planted on the floor."

10. Ask, "May I get your supplies?"

11. Retrieve the gait belt.

12. Place the gait belt on the resident.

13. Confirm the gait belt is snug and not twisted.

14. Position your right knee inside and left leg outside the resident's right leg.

15. Hold the gait belt with palms up on both sides.

16. Say, "We're going to rock back and forth three times. On the third time, I need you to help me stand you up."

17. Count: "1, 2, 3."

18. Stand the resident.

19. Ask, "Are you okay?"

20. Place hands on the back of the gait belt (palms up).

21. Walk the resident a short distance.

22. Say, "Let's turn around."

23. Turn the resident.

24. Say, "Let's walk back to the chair."

25. Walk the resident back to the chair.

26. Say, "Let's turn around."

27. Turn the resident so their back is facing the chair.

28. Say, "Let's back up until your legs touch the chair."

29. Say, "Now sit back and make sure your hips touch the back of the chair."

30. Remove the gait belt.

31. Ask, "May I put your supplies back?"

32. Place the gait belt in the dirty area.

33. Open the privacy curtains.

34. Open the blinds.

35. Push on the bed to ensure it is locked.

36. Ensure the bed is in the lowest position.

37. Give the resident the call light.

38. Ask, "Do you need anything else?"

39. Ask, "May I go wash my hands?"

40. Go wash your hands.

Common Mistakes to Avoid

× Not confirming whether bed the is locked

× Not checking resident's comfort before and after ambulation

× Holding gait belt incorrectly

× Letting the resident walk unsupported

Skill Complete Checklist

√ Shoes and gait belt properly applied

√ Resident safely assisted into and out of chair

√ Gait belt removed and stored

√ Privacy and hand hygiene maintained

√ Call light left within reach

Helping a resident walk safely builds strength and trust. It is also a test of your attention to detail.

FINAL ONE-PAGE CHECKLIST (CNA SKILLS REVIEW PAGE)

This final checklist pulls together the most essential actions you'll repeat across every skill. Use it the night before your exam, or even right outside the testing center, to ground yourself in what matters most: clear communication, safe technique, and calm presence. This isn't a substitute for practice, but your mental run-through before you step into the room.

Hand Hygiene (Every Skill)

☐ Knock and ask to wash hands

☐ Use soap and water for 20 seconds

☐ Dry completely and turn off faucet with paper towel

Opening Steps

☐ Knock and ask to enter

☐ Greet the resident with name and intent

☐ Ask for permission and explain the skill

☐ Wash hands

☐ Close privacy curtain

☐ Check bed lock and position

During the Skill

☐ Speak clearly and slowly

☐ Give instructions before each touch

- ☐ Ask "Are you okay?" during reps or turns

- ☐ Handle body gently and support joints

- ☐ Keep linens and supplies organized

- ☐ Use barrier towels when needed

- ☐ Maintain modesty and comfort

Closing Steps

- ☐ Reposition and redress resident if needed

- ☐ Place call light in hand

- ☐ Ask, "Do you need anything else?"

- ☐ Open curtain and blinds

- ☐ Recheck bed lock and lowest position

- ☐ Return supplies and dispose of linens

- ☐ Remove gloves and wash hands again

Final Notes

- ☐ Stay calm

- ☐ Think out loud (verbalize all actions)

- ☐ If you forget a step, say: "I'd like to correct something"

- ☐ Confidence counts—breathe and smile

CONCLUSION

Passing the CNA skills exam is more than just earning a title. It's your first step into a profession that is becoming more critical by the day. Whether you're heading into long-term care, hospital work, or home health, what you've learned here will go with you every day. You're not just passing a test. You're stepping into someone's life as a caregiver.

You've practiced each skill. You've visualized the steps. You've learned the flow. Now it's time to bring everything together on exam day. Remember, the test isn't about the perfect score, but to demonstrate your ability to provide safe, clear, and consistent care.

www.ingramcontent.com/pod-product-compliance
Lightning Source LLC
Chambersburg PA
CBHW051330120626
46547CB00016B/2481